The YOUNG NATURALIST'S
Sketchbook

Molly Hashimoto

Pomegranate **kids**
— AGES 3 to 103!

Welcome, young naturalist!

The next time you're out on a walk with your family or friends, bring this journal, a sharp pencil, and a keen eye along with you. Look up, look down, look over and under, then record what you see. Maybe you can spot some of the same animals that artist Molly Hashimoto has illustrated, or maybe you'll find others that are native to your part of the world. If you don't know exactly what an animal is called, try to capture as many details as you can about it. Colors, unique markings, size, sounds, location, and time of day are all interesting details to record in your sketchbook. Then when you get home you can conduct research to find the creature's common name and scientific name.

Happy sketching!

Pomegranate Communications, Inc.
19018 NE Portal Way, Portland OR 97230
800 227 1428 • www.pomegranate.com

Distributed by Pomegranate Europe Ltd.
Unit 1, Heathcote Business Centre, Hurlbutt Road
Warwick, Warwickshire CV34 6TD, UK
[+44] 0 1926 430111 • sales@pomeurope.co.uk

Item No. AA891

© 2015 Molly Hashimoto

Designed by Stephanie Odeh
Printed in Korea

24 23 22 21 20 19 18 17 16 15   10 9 8 7 6 5 4 3 2 1

Introduction

Sketch

Carved block

Print

The block prints in this book were all carved and hand-printed in my home studio, inspired by sketches I've made and photos I've taken outdoors. I take a walk near my house almost every day, and I rarely go out without my digital camera or sketchbook. I have a zoom lens, so I can get good close-ups of birds and animals without having to come so near that I frighten them.

Ducks are some of the best subjects for sketching on the spot—they float in the water, remaining rather still, and it's easy to draw them without all the complications of feet and extended wings. They swim around in flocks, so if one duck turns away, another one will take up the same pose, so you can continue drawing.

For sketching on the spot, I hold my pencil loosely and try to find the geometric shapes that make up a bird or animal's outlines, starting first with a body, then adding a head, legs or wings, and, finally, feet. I make multiple lines so I don't have to worry that each line needs to be perfect right away. Later, I can choose the line that most accurately describes the shape. Then I just erase the ones that aren't quite right.

If I can't draw or paint on the spot, I use my photos later. I look at the display screen on my camera and sketch from that, or I print out my photos and use the hard copies combined with birding field guides.

Sometimes it's fun to draw with a black waterproof marker—there's no erasing, but the drawings you end up with will be very bold and sometimes have a lot more energy than ones that you start with pencil.

—Molly Hashimoto

Cardinal (*Cardinalis cardinalis*)

I saw this male cardinal in a long avenue of elms on Bethesda Terrace in New York City's Central Park. Not only is the park a great place to watch birds, it is one of the most important rest stops on the East Coast migration flight path, though some birds, like the cardinal, are year-round residents.

Date: _____ Animal: _____

Location: _____

Notes: _____

_____

_____

_____

Hairy woodpecker (*Picoides villosus*)

As I walked along a mountain lakeshore, this hairy woodpecker alerted me to his presence by tapping gently on a lodgepole pine. I looked up and watched him circling the trunk in search of insects.

Date: _____ Animal: _____

Location: _____

Notes: _____

_____

_____

_____

Raccoon (*Procyon lotor*)

I encountered the bold raccoon at Union Bay Natural Area in Seattle in broad daylight. He allowed me to take lots of photos of him without showing any fear at all. I think he was almost daring me to come closer, but my zoom lens did that for me!

Date:_____ Animal:_____

Location:_____

Notes:_____

_____

_____

_____

Anna's hummingbirds (*Calypte anna*)

I was so surprised to see two hummingbirds next to each other on this crocosmia because they almost always fight over their favorite plants. They are very territorial! This was a young male and female, and I wonder if they had just fledged from their nest and didn't realize they were supposed to be fighting.

Date: _____ Animal: _____

Location: _____

Notes: _____

_____

_____

_____

California quail (*Callipepla californica*)

I love the dramatic markings on the California quail. I saw a family of them in the wetlands nearby my house and thought it would be really fun to create a landscape behind the male that included California poppies and the foothills where they grow.

Date: _____ Animal: _____

Location: _____

Notes: _____

_____

_____

_____

Mule deer (*Odocoileus hemionus*)

This mother and baby were grazing on the meadows above Cascade Head on the central Oregon coast, where I teach each summer. The meadows are rich with grasses and other forage to help the fawns grow strong during the summer months.

Date:_____ Animal:_____

Location:_____

Notes:_____

_____

_____

_____

Belted kingfisher (*Ceryle alcyon*)

The female belted kingfisher is much more dramatically colored than the male, so I chose to create a print with her as my model. Kingfishers make a rattling cry as they fly across ponds, so even when you can't see them, you will know they are there.

Date:_____ Animal:_____

Location:_____

Notes:_____

_____

_____

_____

Barrow's goldeneye (*Bucephala islandica*)

Usually the goldeneyes are quite shy, but this male let me take lots of photos as he paddled around the wetland pond. I love the males' dramatic black-and-white markings, golden eyes, and big blocky heads. *Bucephala* comes from a Greek word meaning "bull-headed."

Date:_____ Animal:_____

Location:_____

Notes:_____

_____

_____

_____

Eastern cottontail (*Sylvilagus floridanus*)

I saw this rabbit in my mother-in-law's backyard in a Chicago suburb, where she has created a beautiful Japanese garden.

Date: _____ Animal: _____

Location: _____

Notes: _____

_____

_____

_____

_____

Painted turtle (*Chrysemys picta*)

This large specimen was sunbathing at the wetland ponds that I visit near my house. When they first emerge from their winter hibernation at the edge of the pond, they are covered in dead leaves and they look quite messy!

Date: _____ Animal: _____

Location: _____

Notes: _____

_____

_____

_____

American robin (*Turdus migratorius*)

American robins are seen everywhere, and although they are so common, they are always a beautiful, welcome sight. In spring their joyful song, "cheerio, cheerio," wakes me each morning. This robin was getting her fill of berries in October.

Date: _____ Animal: _____

Location: _____

Notes: _____

_____

_____

_____

Western tanager (*Piranga ludoviciana*)

The tanager is the most colorful bird in the West with his scarlet head and yellow breast. I saw this one perched on an alder above the Cascade River, below Eldorado Peak in North Cascades National Park, but I have seen them in the city on several occasions.

Date: _____ Animal: _____

Location: _____

Notes: _____

_____

_____

_____

Red fox (*Vulpes vulpes*)

We woke the fox up from her midday siesta one afternoon in early spring when we were hiking way above the Yellowstone River on Specimen Ridge in Yellowstone National Park.

Date:_____ Animal:_____

Location:_____

Notes:_____

_____

_____

_____

Steller's jay *(Cyanocitta stelleri)*

Steller's jays are the blue jays west of the Mississippi. Their raucous squawks can be heard all over my neighborhood. I entice them into my backyard with peanuts, which they love!

Date:_____ Animal:_____

Location:_____

Notes:_____

_____

_____

_____

Rufous hummingbird (*Selasphorus rufus*)

With their long beaks and tongues, hummingbirds have adapted to extract the nectar from tubular flowers. They especially love the color red, so I try to grow many red and pink flowers with trumpet-shaped blossoms. The rufous are a bit smaller than Anna's hummingbirds, and even more aggressive! Once, both species were fighting in my backyard!

Date:_____ Animal:_____

Location:_____

Notes:_____

_____

_____

_____

Western tiger swallowtail butterfly (*Papilio rutulus*)

Swallowtails visit my backyard garden in July and August. I grow verbena plants, both perennial and annual varieties, because they are among the favorite flowers of butterflies.

Date: _____ Animal: _____

Location: _____

Notes: _____

_____

_____

_____

Great blue heron (*Ardea herodias*)

I often see herons in the city wetlands. They are among the easiest birds to photograph and sketch outdoors because they remain motionless in the shallow water as they peer into it, searching for small fish to catch.

Date: _____ Animal: _____

Location: _____

Notes: _____

_____

_____

_____

Caspian tern (*Sterna caspia*)

These terns were diving and walking along the shore. They are favorites of mine because of their dramatic swooping flight and bright orange bills.

Date:_____ Animal:_____

Location:_____

Notes:_____

_____

_____

_____

Coyote (*Canis latrans*)

I saw the coyote one cold January morning at Union Bay Natural Area in Seattle; we watched each other from a short distance before it disappeared into the woods.

Date:_____ Animal:_____

Location:_____

Notes:_____

_____

_____

_____

American crow (*Corvus brachyrhynchos*)

Crows are the main species of bird that we see in our neighborhood in wintertime. They stay out until almost dark and gather in huge groups before flying off to their nighttime roosts.

Date: _____ Animal: _____

Location: _____

Notes: _____

_____

_____

_____

Scrub jay *(Aphelocoma californica)*

I saw a flash of electric blue in a tree, and I was surprised to find this rare visitor, as scrub jays are native in California and not common so far north as Seattle, where I live.

Date: _____ Animal: _____

Location: _____

Notes: _____

_____

_____

_____

Cascades frog (*Rana cascadae*)

We hiked up to a small lake in the Washington Cascades on a ninety-degree day in August. We were so hot and tired. It was completely worth it to see this frog cooling himself in the shallow mountain pond.

Date:_____ Animal:_____

Location:_____

Notes:_____

_____

_____

_____

Yellow-rumped warbler (*Dendroica coronata*)

I place a suet feeder near my kitchen window in winter to attract hungry birds. Foods like insects and berries are so much scarcer in winter, so the birds are willing to come near to the house. Brightly colored birds are as close as we can get to having flowers in winter.

Date:_____ Animal:_____

Location:_____

Notes:_____

_____

_____

_____

Bobcat (*Lynx rufus*)

Bobcats are thriving in many parts of the United States and are the most common feline in North America. I've never seen one in the wild, so I consulted several field guides and online photographs to create this new image. This bobcat looks just a little bit like a pet cat I had as a child.

Date: _____ Animal: _____

Location: _____

Notes: _____

_____

_____

_____

Mountain bluebird (*Sialia currucoides*)

During autumn in Yellowstone National Park, the colors are all muted golds and greens, but the sight of a brilliant mountain bluebird adds a splash of pure primary blue to the scene.

Date:_____ Animal:_____

Location:_____

Notes:_____

_____

_____

_____

Townsend's chipmunk (*Tamias townsendii*)

These chipmunks are very small and fast. Their favorite food is the seeds inside the Douglas fir cones. I see these chipmunks all the time when I hike in the mountains.

Date:_____ Animal:_____

Location:_____

Notes:_____

_____

_____

_____

Cedar waxwing (*Bombycilla cedrorum*)

Waxwings are perhaps the most beautiful birds in the West, with their dramatic crests and splashes of yellow and scarlet plumage. I often see them atop cedars, as their name suggests, but this male was perched in a grove of alder trees. I know to look up to the tree-tops when I hear their high-pitched "seeeeee" call.

Date: _____ Animal: _____

Location: _____

Notes: _____

_____

_____

_____

Pileated woodpecker (*Dryocopus pileatus*)

The pileated is the largest woodpecker, with a huge crest and bright red markings. The striking contrast between the red and white makes these birds stand out starkly on the sides of tree trunks where they probe with their long bills. Of all the species of birds (which are closely related to dinosaurs), they remind me most of the flying pterodactyls.

Date:_____ Animal:_____

Location:_____

Notes:_____

_____

_____

_____

Striped skunk (*Mephitis mephitis*)

Skunks travel by night, and I've only seen one a few times, though I have smelled them on many occasions!

Date:_____ Animal:_____

Location:_____

Notes:_____

_____

_____

_____

Long-eared owl (*Asio otus*)

We saw this young long-eared owl in a grove of poplars. He didn't seem at all afraid as he gazed at us with his piercing stare.

Date: _____ Animal: _____

Location: _____

Notes: _____

_____

_____

_____

Twelve-spotted skimmer dragonfly (*Libellula pulchella*)

The pond in the park below our house has more dragonfly visitors in August than any other location in Seattle. All varieties are there, including this skimmer.

Date:_____ Animal:_____

Location:_____

Notes:_____

_____

_____

_____

_____

American goldfinch (*Carduelis tristis*)

A birdbath in my backyard is a real bird magnet. Birds like water even more than food at times, such as in winter when everything is frozen, or on a hot day where other water sources are dry.

Date: _____ Animal: _____

Location: _____

Notes: _____

_____

_____

_____

American bison (*Bison bison*)

I saw this herd of bison in the Lamar Valley in Yellowstone National Park on a day in September when the aspens were turning golden.

Date:_____ Animal:_____

Location:_____

Notes:_____

_____

_____

_____

_____

Ruby-crowned kinglet (*Regulus calendula*)

After a heavy snow at the park below my house, I went down in search of birds and discovered this tiny kinglet, who would normally be flitting from branch to branch inside huge conifers. On that cold winter day the kinglet was out in plain sight, risking all to find food.

Date: _____ Animal: _____

Location: _____

Notes: _____

_____

_____

_____

Trumpeter swan (*Cygnus buccinator*)

Swans visit a bay near my house in winter, and I love to see their elegant shapes against the blue water.

Date: _____ Animal: _____

Location: _____

Notes: _____

_____

_____

_____

_____

Woodchuck (*Marmota monax*)

This friendly woodchuck sat up and looked at me in Fort Tryon Park in uppermost Manhattan, which is where my daughter lives in a big apartment building. It's funny to think of New York City being home to a large wild mammal like this one, but wherever there are green spaces and parks, animals can make burrows and find food.

Date:_____ Animal:_____

Location:_____

Notes:_____

_____

_____

_____

Dark-eyed junco (*Junco hyemalis oreganus*)

Juncos spend much of their time on the ground, even building their nests there. They often hop around in low shrubs like this hydrangea.

Date: _____ Animal: _____

Location: _____

Notes: _____

_____

_____

_____

Cougar (*Felis concolor*)

Once while I was walking along Diablo Dam Road in the North Cascades and talking to a friend, a cougar crossed the road right behind us. I love the sinewy grace of the cougar, the largest of the wild cats in North America.

Date:_____ Animal:_____

Location:_____

Notes:_____

_____

_____

_____

Date: _____ Animal: _____

Location: _____

Notes: _____

_____

_____

_____

_____

_____

_____

_____

_____

_____

_____

_____

_____

_____

_____

_____

_____

_____

_____

Date: _____ Animal: _____

Location: _____

Notes: _____

_____

_____

_____

_____

_____

_____

_____

_____

_____

_____

_____

_____

_____

_____

_____

_____

_____

_____

_____

_____

Date: _____ Animal: _____

Location: _____

Notes: _____

Date: _____ Animal: _____

Location: _____

Notes: _____
_____
_____
_____
_____
_____
_____
_____
_____
_____
_____
_____
_____
_____
_____
_____
_____
_____
_____
_____

Date: _____ Animal: _____

Location: _____

Notes: _____

_____

_____

_____

_____

_____

_____

_____

_____

_____

_____

_____

_____

_____

_____

_____

_____

_____

_____

_____

_____

_____

Date: _____ Animal: _____

Location: _____

Notes: _____
_____
_____
_____
_____
_____
_____
_____
_____
_____
_____
_____
_____
_____
_____
_____
_____
_____
_____
_____
_____
_____
_____
_____

Date: _____ Animal: _____

Location: _____

Notes: _____

_____

_____

_____

_____

_____

_____

_____

_____

_____

_____

_____

_____

_____

_____

_____

_____

_____

_____

_____

_____

_____

Date: _____ Animal: _____

Location: _____

Notes: _____

_____

_____

_____

_____

_____

_____

_____

_____

_____

_____

_____

_____

_____

_____

_____

_____

_____

_____

Date: _____ Animal: _____

Location: _____

Notes: _____

Date: _____ Animal: _____

Location: _____

Notes: _____

_____

_____

_____

_____

_____

_____

_____

_____

_____

_____

_____

_____

_____

_____

_____

_____

_____

_____

Date: _____ Animal: _____

Location: _____

Notes: _____

_____

_____

_____

_____

_____

_____

_____

_____

_____

_____

_____

_____

_____

_____

_____

_____

_____

_____

_____

Date: _____ **Animal:** _____

Location: _____

Notes: _____

_____

_____

_____

_____

_____

_____

_____

_____

_____

_____

_____

_____

_____

_____

_____

_____

_____

_____

_____

_____

_____

Date: _____ Animal: _____

Location: _____

Notes: _____
_____
_____
_____
_____
_____
_____
_____
_____
_____
_____
_____
_____
_____
_____
_____
_____
_____
_____
_____

Date: _____ Animal: _____

Location: _____

Notes: _____
_____
_____
_____
_____
_____
_____
_____
_____
_____
_____
_____
_____
_____
_____
_____
_____
_____
_____
_____
_____

Date: _____ Animal: _____

Location: _____

Notes: _____
_____
_____
_____
_____
_____
_____
_____
_____
_____
_____
_____
_____
_____
_____
_____
_____
_____
_____
_____
_____

Date: _____ Animal: _____

Location: _____

Notes: _____

_____

_____

_____

_____

_____

_____

_____

_____

_____

_____

_____

_____

_____

_____

_____

_____

_____

_____

_____

_____

_____

Date: _____ Animal: _____

Location: _____

Notes: _____

Date: _____ Animal: _____

Location: _____

Notes: _____

_____

_____

_____

_____

_____

_____

_____

_____

_____

_____

_____

_____

_____

_____

_____

_____

_____

_____

_____

_____

Date: _____ Animal: _____

Location: _____

Notes: _____

_____

_____

_____

_____

_____

_____

_____

_____

_____

_____

_____

_____

_____

_____

_____

_____

_____

_____

_____

_____

Date: _____ Animal: _____

Location: _____

Notes: _____
_____
_____
_____
_____
_____
_____
_____
_____
_____
_____
_____
_____
_____
_____
_____
_____
_____
_____
_____
_____
_____
_____

Date: _____ Animal: _____

Location: _____

Notes: _____
_____
_____
_____
_____
_____
_____
_____
_____
_____
_____
_____
_____
_____
_____
_____
_____
_____
_____
_____
_____
_____
_____
_____

Date: _____ Animal: _____

Location: _____

Notes: _____
_____
_____
_____
_____
_____
_____
_____
_____
_____
_____
_____
_____
_____
_____
_____
_____
_____
_____
_____
_____
_____

Date: _____ Animal: _____

Location: _____

Notes: _____
_____
_____
_____
_____
_____
_____
_____
_____
_____
_____
_____
_____
_____
_____
_____
_____
_____
_____
_____
_____

Date: _____ Animal: _____

Location: _____

Notes: _____
_____
_____
_____
_____
_____
_____
_____
_____
_____
_____
_____
_____
_____
_____
_____
_____
_____
_____
_____
_____
_____

About Molly Hashimoto

Molly Hashimoto (American, b. 1951) is on a mission to connect people to nature through her art. Sketchbook and camera in hand, she explores the wild areas of the western United States to create prints and paintings of the abundant flora and native wildlife in their natural habitat. Her colorful scenes reflect a keen eye, an easy closeness to her surroundings, and a deep regard for all creatures great and small. Near her home in the Pacific Northwest, she may encounter a resting great blue heron, an ambling raccoon, or a territorial hummingbird. She captures these moments with sketches or photographs, later turning them into woodblock prints or watercolors.

Teaching is an important part of her artistic journey. In addition to the outdoor seminars that she teaches for the North Cascades Institute, the Yellowstone Association Institute, and the Sitka Center for Art and Ecology, she also offers programs for King County Library System and Sno-Isle Library System.

When she is not hiking, creating, or teaching, she's writing about art and nature at www.mollyhashimoto.com.